THE SONG THE ORIOLE SANG

First published in 2010 by
The Dedalus Press
13 Moyclare Road
Baldoyle
Dublin 13
Ireland

www.dedaluspress.com

ISBN 978 1 906614 30 0

Dedalus Press titles are represented in North America by
Syracuse University Press, Inc., 621 Skytop Road,
Suite 110, Syracuse, New York 13244,
and in the UK by
Central Books, 99 Wallis Road, London E9 5LN

Cover image 'Li River at Dawn' © KingWu/iStockphoto.com

The Dedalus Press receives financial assistance from
The Arts Council / An Chomhairle Ealaíon

THE SONG THE ORIOLE SANG

Philip McDonagh

Matthew and Alison

Love

from

Philip

Irish Embassy London

5 Nov. 2010

DEDALUS PRESS
DUBLIN, IRELAND

ACKNOWLEDGEMENTS

Acknowledgements are due to the editors of the following in which poems from this collection, or versions of them, were previously published: *The Irish Times* and *Poetry Ireland Review*.

for my wife Ana
whose love
has brought these poems
into the light

Contents

7

PART FIVE

PART SIX – HELSINKI

PART SEVEN

Mo Díreach

IT LED US to a thing we never did
the cutting newspapers to save the tributes—
as if the lapidary could conserve
módh díreach

the Imperial Hotel:
Mo suddenly mandated
everyone who had a care for Ireland
rallied from bed-and-breakfast land
me in my suit crumpling the coverlet—
until Mo takes my glass
unbidden sips my white wine
asks what my brain tells me

the London Embassy:
her stockinged feet propped on puffed cushions
she calls the PM "Tony"
her worry, who'll be listened to
in the great elbow-driven conclave

a borrowed plane:
Mo writing one-line thank yous
all the dusky way
from Warrington of the Sorrows—
for she can do this much

that house in Islington
she and Jon will leave eventually:
Mo coming from the House of Commons late
roast beef home-cooked
each word indicative

stichomythia of me with David Frost
enacting the ephemera
that in a year that was
made me love England
And one more thing, Butterling:
get the ferret out of the elephant's cage,
it doesn't fool anyone

My-name-is-little-Alan-Price
I've-tried-to-be-nice-all-my-life
resounds in the upper room

and at the summit of the wheel
is written Hecuba
Mo Secretary of State
the One Untumoured

a walnut table then
and Mo in metamorphosis
is asking our advice
on whether a date certain for negotiations
will meet with a Republican response

a prison cot
Mo in her loose wig
plays cards with paramilitaries—
or is it snakes and ladders
with fallen women

or chess with angels
for all she minds our curiosity
for all she can imagine
the endeavour's end?

later in Hammersmith
in that small garden
bestridden by the tiny feet
of Star the guinea hen
she and Jon set out ideas
by now unmarketable
on high finance
the Baghdad bombs and Brown

a man divorced
saves his few quid to take a five-year-old
of whom he hasn't custody
for early fish-and-chips
on Saturday:
that windy spell along the sea-front
is what our greatness is, Mo says,
and why she is or was a politician

her bravest Blackpool style
would flash illuminations:
in India
she spares herself on stairs

the rest is not quite silence

the fullest of full houses
in Drury Lane
Neil Kinnock, Adam Ingram, and Clare Short
thanks-giving for her life

roof-raising on their feet
a Labour century behind them
have all of us arise
whom her life touched
not for 'Jerusalem'
but for the anti-anthem
of an unformed age
'Always look on the bright side of life'

as if with some unseen yet burning bow
we're chasing ferrets
out of history's elephant cage—
and I and Chris Smith
the theatre still swirling in communion
become aware
of what is not alluded to
of something almost expelled
that in Mo's anthem nonetheless recurs

freeze-framed on Golgotha
eternally off-message
three ersatz trees

INDIA

Essential Things

for Tara, aged 1 year 9 months

Most Mamas don't let things occur
just so: they have a rule.
She'll want to move you—nudge
you on or even pull you after her
into the babies' pool.
Don't budge.
The essential thing is, keep flat
your hand, and splash! Like that,

sitting like this. The things
a Mama knows for definite!
You're wearing water wings,
you're at the edge, you have a go at it,
at least try, swimming. Mind,
the next essential thing is, be kind:
you finally give in.
But as soon as you begin,

be like a whale that owns the whole sea,
or else the perky little fish
cosy as can be
inside the whale's tummy. Do as you wish,
borrow the other children's floats—
whatever. Mama dotes,
and other Mamas tell their lot
what's what.

But if your Mama tries to lift you out,
I mean ahead of time,
the essential thing is this:
a Big Shout
is No Crime.
Not too much thinking though—you'll miss
the splashing. One—two—three.
Hand flat. Follow me.

Alumna

Our little one steps free,
Places her turtle sideways
To the darkening sea.
The creature, having no guide
But creature-knowledge, finds her fins,
Senses which way the sea is.

My eyes on Tara's eyes, I see
Sarat the hatchery-man
Bestow on her a pineapple:
His barns are full
And she the Plenipotentiary
Of Innocence's Land.

What help can we provide,
If once the rushing and retreating tide
That knows no hurt
Snatch up our turtle?
What helpline can we open
To the submarine,
If to the gullet of the ocean
She goes down, a dorsal
Shadow? And Leviathan
With twist of trunk and pink tongue
Buries a sweet morsel?

They say green turtles,
Living with luck a hundred years or more,
Come back in all their generations
To one shore;

As festivals
That fill our wells
Of commonality
And make new marriages,
Are bigger than ourselves
And yet consist,
As flesh fails, world ebbs,
In only us; our tryst.

The orange sun,
Black cloud, and shifting sea
Merge. Their colours run,
And night's drape falls.

A hundred years on,
Also our little Tara will have gone.
I see her children's children come
To hear the Lankan marriage drum
With children of their own
And praise the dancers wearing beehive crowns
And elephants in homespun
Grandeur plodding the shoreline!
Whether America's the bigger gun
Or China—may it not impinge
On turtle- or on toddler-dom!
They wade, by night, by day, on golden sand.

A little helmet bobs within the waves.
Can we accompany in thought
Our soft-shelled creature,
Spinning in sea-water
As the homeward bee braves
Wind, a rudderless Argonaut?

May she return,
Our foster turtle,
To coconut and palm
Warming their roots in sand!
Just here,
Our lucent moon,
A lost balloon
Beyond the sea's perimeter,
Within the world's womb
Floats near,
Is twinned with stars!

I hold a small hand,
As careful not to crumple it
As if on the indefinite,
Arduous night-strand,
I had ensconced
A sprig that fell once,
Imprescribably,
From the primeval tree.

The moment ends.
"Bye-bye," she waves, "Bye-bye."
A lopsided friendship—
To me a butterfly
On Time's whale's back
Or signet of the realm
That when rhymes crack
Will overwhelm
One day, Tara and me,
Us two who tread the verge
Of the immeasurable sea,
As castles made of sand slowly submerge.

The Usual Drill

They come to kill.

Usurping on the jungle,
they make of others
polishers of guns, porters of toilets,
beaters in the long grass.
Their licensed enemy
is that soft-peddling parti-coloured shadow,
the king of mordancy,
whose burning eye moves pens.

The usual drill.

They keep their tallies in a cursive script
on boards, and pose for pictures.
Their business is self-portraiture:
as if invented purpose
yielded valency,
as if a photograph could ask,
'Did Hercules heroically handle
a quarry more richly strange?'

What role do I fulfil?

I smile and do not sing.
They want a poetry cut down
to proclamation,
jingle and drum,

a tale to solemnise
their poor shenanigans
whose ends are means,
a subaltern success.

Of which the chance is nil.

Kerala

I shall remember Kerala
for how the disappearing moon
glanced in our faces, as if the sea
not far from Kottayam, in which
we watched for birds, was there by destiny.

The singing in the temples would begin
too early—in darkness
the caterpillar of the mind
can dream itself a butterfly.
The doorways of the churches,
boxing pale gold,
intruded on the universe of sleep.

I shall remember Kerala
for the emptying of silence,
as if the stirring of hens, the coffee
women carried to their men
in battered cups, fulfilled a destiny.

The world rolls on:
the coughing trucks
painted like dancers,
the coconut trees ideally tall,
the crows' reconnaissance
of still water,
humanity at hazard
along the road's edge,
the rumoured strike not happening.

I shall remember Kerala
for the cantilever of the sky
at noon, as if a great marquee
hoisted by a well-wisher beyond
the world's far rim, explained our destiny.

At Mararíkulam,
our little daughter playing on the beach
met up with someone else's little one,
a pair as serendipitous
as dolphins following a boat—
and Anthony, who worked at the hotel,
would show us everything:
the vegetable garden,
the water filter of a modern kind,
the staff canteen.

I shall remember Kerala
because the serious money's gone
north—aerospace no industry
for people cherishing their fruits
and coconuts like seeds of destiny.

Where spread a Latin bishopric
before the coming of the caravels,
the hoardings have news
of Hutch and Hyundai,
of biscuits, weddings, and gold,
or speak with infinite assurance
of the Catholic Syrian Bank
and how Karishma's face
miraculously entertains
the multitude
on cable television.

Even the highway's free
with personal advice:
*Hurry is Worry. Left is Right,
Don't mix Drink with Drive.*

I shall remember Kerala
for unobtrusive ambling
in the streets of Allepey,
as if to find silk for a wedding
in far-off time fulfilled a destiny.

A mother prays for safety
for a daughter cutting vegetables
in the spotless kitchens
of a too-much dreamt-of land.
For school-books for his little son,
a fisherman implores the sea.
All business is unfinished at the end,
no ledger evened up by evening-time.
This ancient land will celebrate as yet
the necessary innocence of the crib
and of the king's return.

I shall remember Kerala
for the simple star that guided us
at dawn: the taxi's filigree,
needle-and-thread work in the streets
of old Cochin, affirmed our destiny.

Burning Bright

The science is to wait.
Here at a dusty crossing of the roads,
expecting contact
with our elemental prince,
we pass round binoculars.
A deer's cry in the forest,
the monkeys in cahoots, all frantic;
then the supervening roar,
that absolute insistence,
as in the footage,
presaging a fierce bolt:
the orange ornament
of our deciduous world.

We wait some more, pull out our shawls.
Then almost silence.
The faint suggestions of the doves,
nature's unanswered telephone.
A crocodile by water,
dead-like as the root
of the gnarled banyan.
Engines revved up, the jeeps move on,
running their track
in a retracting light.
The park will close,
absent our beast-celebrity,
lord of the melee of nature.

I would acquire
a textual acquaintance with the leaves.
I would acknowledge
the incorrigible modesty
of flame-in-the-forest
and flights of parakeets
that spread in synchrony
in the sufficient light
to settle all-in-one,
a peacock's tail.

The *chhatri* on a slope,
so courteous in its address to nature,
reminds me,
a breeze among the pillars,
of who observes,
of someone's and of all our passing.

Women at the Well

For a splash of sweet water
women await their turn
right up to night's fall
as undemonstrative
as if they stood
kiln-hardened and slack-bellied
in that curved line of jars:
green dresses, pink tops, and orange veils
as gallant as flesh on bone.

Reflections on a Rajput Fortress

If causes of four centuries ago
are not remembered now,
why pillage a warm nest
to make a soldiery?

I write no elegy but note merely
revetements eternally redundant,
dead claws embracing couch grass,
a monkeys' gymnasium.

Kessel

An engineer I met in India
had come to water-tanks, a chosen work,
on his discovering that more than half
our engineering brains go round in a circle

improving motor cars. This was no edict
against cars as such. The "but" or "if"
was where to place them in the bigger picture
of mankind driving smoothly off the cliff

of natural limit. At Stalingrad, too, oil
was part of the whole thing. In the *Kessel,*
he told me, the half-million faced it all
with discipline. They fought and functioned, wrestling

their local angels: madness in the Bunker
magicked a massive struggle into junk.

The Singer of Allepey

for Shashi Kapoor, Shakespeare-wallah

"I once was a wild shoot
of bamboo, now am flute:
play and play on I must
until my wood is dust."

The singer—favourite star
of Indian cinema—
to sing at Allepey
this night will take no fee.

"Once, an abandoned shoot
of bamboo became flute.
Though chance may snap the cane,
still will the song remain."

The scene an orphanage.
The children's looks assuage
the sickness in his blood.
Moon floats on the night's flood.

"I once was a wild shoot
of bamboo, now am flute:
play and play on I must
until my wood is dust."

The News from India

for S.G., May 2004

Why does it clutch the heart
as if some long adultery were over
and a household cleansed?

And what do I intend,
consorting in a region of the clouds
in this old part

of Dublin? How to explain
elation—that a message on my cell
about returns

from polling districts churns
memories, and a late monsoon's abandon
swirls in this rain?

MEMORIES OF AN IONIAN DIPLOMAT

THE AMBASSADOR WAS up at dawn
in the large famous house
and grumbled at the ineffectual fan
as he started to compose.
Soon he would retire—
another costume change,
a last improvisation.
The sheeting of the late monsoon
ghosted his old villa.
A youthful cornucopia,
half-memory, half-dream—
rain streeling on the pavement
in a fallow time,
through open doors
the bells of bicycles that floated in,
a pollinating sound—
displaced abiding properties
within himself. It seemed,
within that evanescent womb
of India,
to have stayed at home to teach Greek verbs
had been best recompense
of parents' love; had made most sense.

THESE LETTERS, in any case,
he thought of as atoms in a void,
as per Democritus,
each destined differently.
Another Constitution would come up
for Europe and its Union.
According to those most in touch
with Brussels, a job like this,
or just like this,
might not need doing again—
he wrote on in a careful hand,
for no real reason he could understand.

SOME DAILY PAPERS were brought in,
touched at the edges by rain.
The readers of the Age of Hindustan
could not stand very much
that wasn't unreality,
in which last category belonged
today's main revelation:
"ultimate prompt global reach
capability"—
what Aristotle termed
Omnipresence and Omnipotence,
and others more recently the Supergun—
was on the way,
the weapons out for tender—
this morning then,
a time for handwriting,
for clearances and acts of self-doubt,
through which no boundaries would be pushed out.

THE DEPUTY HEAD bearer,
thin-armed in giant sleeves,
brought coffee in a canister;
and from the scudding rain,
a mali, barefoot, damp flowers.
Dancers in prose form,
they seemed inevitable,
holding their own
beyond employment
and beyond what comradeship
the fusing rain let slip.

BEFORE I LEAVE, the Ambassador resolved,
I'll call Harinder, my head man,
and ask him not,
"Are all these people necessary?"
as queried by the services at home,
but rather, if in so much duty done,
desire comes into it;
if ever the benefactions of the rain,
the virtuosity of early flowers,
trip up his mood, as mine;
and in the sweepings and re-sweepings
may be discerned
some prompt of *eros;*
or smooth *agápe*
in gleaming plates and glass.
Philía, that fine friendship
Greeks and Romans found
among the well-connected,
seems in any case ruled out.

And as for family,
Harínder, being a widower
without a village,
doesn't find,
most likely, comfort of that kind.

DID NOT OUR predecessor,
old Megasthenes—
the thought fell out of heaven
like the rain itself—
find himself similarly stumped
by the life-absorbing roles
of Indian servants?
Did he not see
in caste a system like Greek slavery?

THE AMBASSADOR,
heart plangent as the rain,
worked on within the deep-mined privacy
of composition. From him
and his imagining his friends,
no catapult or city-wall,
no nuclear device
or confrere of the bunker-busting sun,
would splendidly arise,
on Cyclopean slabs of enterprise!

WITHIN THE VOID,
his disconnectedness, thought came
that comes the same to all men—
the after-phenomenon
Hippolytus must have known
treading spring grass, or Socrates
the day he never gave the mob
the death-sentences they craved
for Arginusae—and already
the hemlock was being stirred,
the sun sinking over Hymettus,
audible the dirge of bees—
and then he seems to hear Megasthenes.

IONIAN-BORN,
a European diplomat
at Pataliputra,
he's seen enough, Megasthenes,
of what a pike would do to men's bowels,
of Alexander and his companions,
princes who never understood
the curvature of the earth
or that their Macedonians,
each man a king to his own child,
would always want home.
In dripping Afghan tents,
or bivouacked off-map in Bactria,
those princes were the axioms
of every proposition,
their great Selefkia
as little Babylonian, to speak
the truth, as Macedonians were Greek.

BUT THERE ARE things much worse—
on this Megasthenes insists—
than life lived out of context.
One does what needs doing
in such a circumstance,
cutting the cloth exactly.
One summers out monsoons
with chicks and canopies.
Meanwhile one tests quite thoroughly the wine
and probes a little the philosophers
sent by the Macedonian royals
in their changing hierarchies
to Chandragupta Maurya.
Avoiding fuss,
one branches out. One reads Herodotus.

SEALING HIS LETTERS
as the sated rains
rise from their garden bed,
the Ambassador dreams
perhaps he too will write,
or frame a memory that someone else,
a Clement or an Arrian
to his Megasthenes, will note down;
and in two thousand years, as monsoon rain
makes paradise
of plain lawns, ordinary trees,
the spade of time will turn it up, this thought,
a shard conjured of earth,
a sharp-edged atom tumbling through the void
to catch Intelligence's
common inextinguishable light—

a marriage in a cave
of speck with spark—
and set aflame
in some tired other heart
adrift on life's margins
that aforementioned after-phenomenon
in the lea of feeling
where sentiment becomes much blurred,
for which the Greeks could never find a word.

Rome

Annunciation

Let me always remember,
if not full facts,
a point at which the search for memories
can start again: in this case,

a table-cloth white as for baptism
the drop of olive oil in hot bean soup
water *frizzante*
conversation pure.

We had repaired, to use that old word,
to a *trattoria*
no more than a short stroll from the Uffizi.
January was bright,

habitual words broke beautiful as bread.
Concourse with Leonardo,
Venus in her shell courting no touch,
had beached us beyond anguish.

How Jennifer in Canada
was ready for the birth of Betty-Ann's
and Don's new grand-child
a cell-phone suddenly announced.

Those breaking waters, were they close or far
from Florence and her statues—
those contemplated rains
embracing dry banks,

the current carrying as on a raft
of rushes one breathing child?
"Whose birthday then?" A waiter waves
the *conto*, all hands reach out.

A mother's helpless and holy prayer
before a struggling candle
and on his cross a *contadino* Christ
maestro of value-added

for Ana and me
are as a portal opening: from here
not memory merely but what is prism
and coronal of memory runs on—

we paused in the piazza,
two pigeons perching on bronze Cosimo;
and having found our feet
in the gigantic world, were free to go.

The Song the Oriole Sang

As if our Dante Alighieri
in his *Purgatorio* or *Paradiso*
went on about a recipe
for *puttanesca*,
or recommended a *Nearco* wine,
why, in long lines
and many volumes, does Bai Juyi
recount for us particulars
of boiling up bamboo shoots
with rice, and how,
on waking from his nap late afternoon,
he took two cups of special tea?

He was a mandarin
who governed provinces,
was sometimes in and sometimes out,
but in the midst of this he tells us more
about the price of peonies
twelve hundred years ago
in the Imperial City,
about the song the oriole sang
as the administrator paused
from drafting papers,
than anything those papers might have said.

So I had thought,
until I saw the commentary in portraits:
self-mutilating soldiers,
the woman gleaning the grain
her family must live off,
the old farm labourer who bows his head

passing the flower-stall, to think,
"A cluster of deep-red flowers
would pay the tax of a whole family."

So now, within vicissitude,
I study with Bai Juyi
the frontier-free coherent universe
of plum-tree or cherry-branch,

would strive with him
towards temples
air-cooled by altitude
at six days' walk from the familiar river

or stop—for what
to peasant or poet pausing here
a thousand years before
the river magisterially gave.

Touching the Stones

"All morning we looked round and around the citadel…"
 —George Seferis, 'The King of Asine'

A day of smooth summer sailing
the Athenians came, their sea-power
inestimable, oars flailing,
Phoenicia's golden name outshone,
even great Persia under restraint.
The Delians looked wonderingly on,
their long wait over, as the galley's oars,
impudent in white paint,
were stilled, in every mouth rich Nikias.
I see him—steady hand and faring
so well. That he should safely pass,
reserved, dark-robed, in bearing
suggesting the indispensable
character of an as yet
unshaken greatness, Protocol
Police, all functionaries, fret and sweat.

The Stoa is on a sudden extant,
as if not all our purposes are bent
by time; and though the centuries,
since Nikias's day of grace,
have massed up, as we slowly stare,
no need of archaeology,
child's play to see that over there
stood once the giant bronze palm tree.

My finger on the stones, another clear
picture presents: fresh mud,
the hoplites, a rabble, gobbling water
red with the newly cheapened blood
of brothers—the banks too sheer
to climb, men penned for slaughter
because the order for withdrawal
from Syracuse had come too late.
Our Nikias had gambled all
on a famous personal equation
with Fortune. To die so soon,
for one who could engage
heaven, was never meant; more sage
to wait on the full moon.

Delos, all rubble and suggestion.
The Aegean sun playing its banjo
on the disjointed stones. My quest
completed as they move a stanchion.
"NIKIAS"—cut clean and straight:
a lettering to make the whole world wait.

Anamnesis at Agrigento

THE RECTILINEAR GIVES WAY

among the olive trees
old stones are thrown like dice

a lizard apt in the sun
has re-aligned himself

in another element
remote cathedral bells

roll and are spent.

ACROSS THIS ROCK'S RIM

at twenty-six or -seven
I saw the universe

an olive beauty taught me
untouchability

so strong youth's cup, to live
was plenitude, events

never definitive.

GLAZED ARE THE SEA'S HIGHWAYS

horizon on horizon
to Africa's green coast

smooth off the wheel, the future's
calyx as capable

of hope as when the waves'
dance dazzled and deceived

poor Carthaginian slaves.

ADRIAN HAS MOVED ON

randomly to the temple.
Though it be obvious

to lend a personal
shoulder to time's harness

and follow, a tug perceived
as unavoidable

would have me not leave.

here where the Muse whispers
a quadrant formed by shade

and silence will permit
a poem's parabola

life's parts inhere
in equilibrium

all in the one sphere.

Party Piece

Whatever this extra is, the making
of poems, tonight in Carraroe
we're as we find ourselves. Re-fill
the glasses, give small ones the thrill
of staying up late. Our time together
is like the *craiceann clocha* growing

without attention on stone walls,
or the sequential blackberries
ripening in the gorse—a shambles
of family, love's loose preamble:
Silence for Diya, hair made up
in bunches, doing her party-piece!

Oven-gold

Neruda would compare us poets
to local bakers, our hands full
with neighbours' needs. As poems are rolled
and baked, what turns to oven-gold
and gives life, has a simple beauty,
rising in the artisanal.

Out of the ordinary, a poem
accomplished is the counterpart
or echo of the source, yet fixed
for good, an element unmixed:
a star the pinioned prisoner sees,
names, and is comforted at heart.

The Dying Alpino

Beneath a pale rose-window in the cathedral,
a teacher is telling her fifteen year-olds
about their local poet. Little heeding
how his art had "disappointed the whole world,"
mundum delusit; even less impressed
that Jacopone, following St. Francis,
was thought a fool, a *stultus propter Christum,*
they must endure this Latin that by chance
descends to them. Her gentle voice impinges:
"a fool, but on account of Christ." The immense
idea is levered up—a siege-engine
to assail the girdle of their diffidence.

A restaurant, by name the *Fonte Cesia.*
Todi, the same day. Mid-symposium.
Alfredo, eighty-five, on a carafe
of white wine. By permission of her mum,
Diya, at three the youngest of our circle,
on Fanta. Pasta in a dish of porcelain
to feed five thousand. Something now at work
in and among us—and as once the wine
and chickpeas, the wood's death into flame,
prompted a poet to ask his visitor,
"How old were you the summer the Mede came?"
I turn to ask Alfredo about the war.

"A so-called hospital. A young Alpino
was in the neighbouring bed, almost erased
from this world. Officers—a type I'd seen,
up from Saló—were leaning over, praising
the Fascists. If he would sign, they were offering
him food, the journey home. My starving soldier,
I should explain, had sworn no oath to the King.
And so the *Commissario* got bolder:
'And you will see your mother.' From that bed
under a grimy window-pane, three words,
'*preferisco-morire-qua,*' stay in my head:
a foolishness not in the end absurd."

The Traveller Considers a Photograph
of His Daughters

Beside my bed,
a print-out of two little ones in red,
their faces radiant,
as if their heads being sideways, bent,

part-touching, stirred
in each their small hearts an absurd
confidence. I fall
to my pyjamaed knees, and all

that real estate
of night-time will not separate
me from them, nor distress
discolorate this emptiness.

Here, now, they stand,
safe in my prayers. Unlimited, this land
where tall swans glide
on ambling rivers. Country-wide,

fruit-trees repair
decorously their losses. Dare
as they will, and stray,
and even when we others drop away

and a dour part
is played by circumstance, two princess-hearts,
acceding to this place,
will wear the circlet: here lives love's embrace.

Assisi Railway Station

No master of Assisi, Cimabue
or Giotto, would have done this damp, cold
morning—a life earth-bound, a smudged cartoon,
politeness to the taxi-man place-holding

for payment in cash. In the station bar,
dragging your un-wheeled suitcases this far,
you cling to a drained cup for company.
The migrant workers clear last night's debris

from the unlived-in platform. A machine
franks tickets. Then, as if to make all well
by force of sheer clanging and re-design
your day, comes Porciuncula's first bell:

the tired mind's tallying you leave below
to find St. Francis on Subasio.

Sleeping in the Cave

She was the music in a fairy-tale
abruptly ended. Single, he will go,
greet in his grief the city's white first flowers,
the aconites. Those baby fists break snow,
but miracles that were the bread and honey once
within two conjoined lives are blank, a code

un-signifying. And if memories
of her last hours and words when once arisen
stavelessly tumble, time to put in order
the empty flat. Let patience make of prison
a hermitage. For to repose on rock,
the breastbone or the bosom of what is,

this too is bravery—a listening,
as Lotte would have wished, for some new thing.

The Tricycles

Like Lydian treasure,
tricycles for sale:
a cornucopia
of the mechanical.
A seat-belt for the doll
thrown in as well,
and with its rippling sound
a *campanello.*

Piazza Navona's river deities,
posing in post-card mode and pride of place,
are not more classically Rome than these
tricycles on the cobble-stones, the grace
of black street-vendors, this *pistaccio*
ice-cream for which the lady in the shop
is undercharging us, or the side-show
of pigeonly altercation and hip-hop.

A woman officer
astride a horse admits
within one smile the majesty
of two small tricyclists.
All the crude coinage
of news broadcast in bits,
the sport, scandal, and catastrophe,
this radiance resists.

Our Lady of the Sand

A panther constituted for the poet
Rilke, without rules in the wilderness,
weary of wayfaring, something definite,
a fact, no mere emotional excess;
hence his commitment to describing it.

Among the shadows of the ancient church
we married in, Our Lady's named *ten-Zavel,*
"built by a sandy place," into my search
for affirmation in the dark side-chapel
of shuttling worry, self-directed cavilling,

parades the panther—his raw sheen, the wood
of the true cross in Piero della Francesca,
a Queen down on her knees as if to ask
how one beam's gleam is be understood
within the run of things, if it bodes good;

his beauty, bursting the frame of symmetry,
resembling what the reasonable hands
of ancient guilds once promised in loft and spandrel,
in sequencing and connectivity
among the images. This apple-tree

alive with cognate blossom, this opened gate
for the *ommegang* of us-not-quite-ourselves
to come to the one fold, contests our fate
and the interstices that separate
one person from another. Here are salved,

in gist, the self-same hurts. Enabled here
is neither the rare breeding that will hatch
a right reaction; nor soul's meteor
gesture; nor how to hasten on the crutch
of shrewdness and push out competitors.

Among these candles is beauty's privilege
to astound in the occasional, resource
ventures off-map; to vivify the sparse,
the lingering. We too fixed our lives' portion
before Our Lady, plunging on a pledge.

Under the Orange Trees

A thing so beautiful
could only be a blessing:
this embroidered rug
spread on fresh grass
under the orange trees,
the superfluous white blossom.

No gathering swallows here,
no grounded albatross of a poet
wearing his ill fate
like an unseasonable overcoat.

Yet it goes hard, dear love,
that what your hands made beautiful,
the trees' roof,
the blackbird-welcoming branch,
are ours only by accident,
a floreat as of the momentary plant
that once protected Jonah,

and we are nothing in Nineveh.

SAVING THE BALLOONS

A sequence of poems for Mrs. Aruna Kumar,
Honorary Secretary of the Delhi Council for
Child Welfare, *in memoriam*

I — AGENT OF THE FACTS

Here in this wall, this crevice, day or night,
a basket takes the weight of a small body.
This tugs a bell inside the orphanage.
Nigel is eighty, veteran of the Raj,
escort on our descent to the street-life
of Mughal Delhi, agent of the facts.
A child's given up, without a name or papers.
But then a door, a hatch within the wall,
opens. A seeming after-thought, our short
detour off Alipur Road. Not to compare
with mosque, haveli, fort. With public legend,
sultans, Qudsia Bagh. Yet straw-hatted
Nigel has found for us a different music.
A little one abandoned is taken in.

Palna begins for us peripherally
that Christmas, with Yvonne's left-over money.
Mrs. Kumar—Aruna—welcomes us,
minus all rhetoric. Over sugary tea,
unscripted time will speak the miracle:
so much material for tears and yet
these happy children. Later, a whole Department
contributes out of payslips to support
a clinic for new-borns. A prejudice
that second-best for lovelorn little ones
should not be thought enough builds Tír na n-Óg,
the orphanage's playground. An unplanned
journey is guided to the royal road
by chance: as Muses draw down carelessly
a measure from the incorrigible spheres.

III — A RUINED ORCHARD

*I am the light of no man's eye, to rival
no one, support no one. I am a song
not capable of rending hearts; a lost
fortune; an orchard ruined, without hope
under this lower heaven. Who so rich
in prayer as to bring flowers at my going,
light up my lamp?* So sings the emperor,
Bahadur Shah, defeated in the game.
A child abandoned to the orphanage
will cling, her eyes averted and unseeing,
to wrapping paper torn at the edge,
its gloss all crumpled, biscuits all now gone,
her poor viaticum; a mother's broken
offering, the most she had; a last *prasad.*

Our invitation is to all the children
of walking age, from 2 right up to 9,
for children's theatre, a banana-guzzling
elephant in the forecourt, Indian-style
tea: Limca, cakes, pakoras on green lawns.
At sundown, time to go, Aruna's word
"height-wise" unites them quickly. Two year-olds
jostle in front, the elders trip along
behind—the one peculiarity,
the saving the balloons and clutching them,
even off doors and trees. As they progress,
filtering on board an old wheeled hulk, we wave:
like jewels wrapped in straw, at every window,
small faces gleaming in a balloon-sea.

V — A Just God's Footprint

A Saturday night concert to raise funds,
so many guests, our flower-borders tremble.
The trays go round, we huddle. Prophesying
above the band, composed in his white turban,
the chief commissioner predicts that barefoot
voters will, as in the Emergency,
remember the Mahatma. Images
of Palna segue. Near the screen, I find
the usual Aruna, brisk, brown sari,
allowing the work to speak. But something gives.
*I don't accompany them now—not since
returning once from Italy, I cried
the whole way.* The hub-bub our silent womb,
a just God's footprint lights upon the earth.

Bird-noises in the early morning garden.
The scattering red petals of the rose
will not disturb her sleep, nor the slow flow
of Yamna's river as the bier is brought
to the cremation-ground. The cloth is lifted,
her daughters kiss the face. A chant, a pouring
of water round, and then the inevitable:
before the ghee and flames, they smash the pot.
Whose is the care of potsherds? Out of range,
a solitary bundle dumped in death's
basket by night is passing through the wall,
only our sketched-out prayers to follow her.
May she awake, as once in questing days
her children woke, into the arms of love.

HELSINKI

Poetics

In writing poems, an endless question
is whether elbowing a space
clear in the midst of family
and friends is any guarantee
of good work: dynamism, drive,
won't substitute a given grace.

I've lived through fifty-six good years.
My hair is not yet, not quite, grey.
Nothing is now inevitable:
being overweight, or taken ill,
not being promoted, mid-wiving
new poems to the light of day.

Nor can I say that orbiting
Ireland for years is by design.
We live without an obvious
fall-back: no dreamt-of, big-enough house
for things we've saved up, our ideas
and books, accumulated wine.

My one proviso: that first move
reaching beyond obedience
must be protected. Poems are done
the way the wind-wise halcyon,
her wing her augury, abides
weather, waits on the sea's good sense.

Lapland

When law backed up by legions
channels the truth,
what makes community?

When all is leverage and lucre
and networked in,
can song and psalm break free?

Laconic Lappish landscapes
of lakes, trees, rock—
how is it they display

a fantail subtlety, as if
a master's touch
found every shade in clay?

In vastness, abacuses
are lost for beads,
and mere derivatives

of will crash. We shall verify
in bog, brook, fell, flower
a handiwork that lives.

The Sampo

Ilmarinen, the master smith,
more able in technology
than policy, went shinnying
into the pine-tree to lay hold
of Moon and Great Bear where the poet
pictured them, resting in its crown;
and so was taken by the wind,
shouldered to dreary Pohjola.

Of swan's plumes, barren heifers' milk,
he forged a great machine against
Famine and Frost, his not-a-plough
so difficult of description,
milling and minting corn, salt, coins.
But the gold-belted girl they said
was his cried off. With head down-hung
he sailed home, smith Ilmarinen.

The unsatisfactory doesn't
end here; for they stuck that machine
deep in the mountain, its output
so bound to one place and people,
it brought war. The thing got smashed, sunk,
splinters are what is left: wood-huts,
our scouring lakes for fish the length
of a brief summer, barley bread.

You, poet, for all your spellbinding,
your songs, your jaw-bone harp, your spars
wielded as weapons, bloodlessly—
you were for killing Marjatta's child:
hopes of a comprehensible
Great Mill, of un-bargained for love
abundant in the gathering place
of the young, squashed like red berries.

Outside the Cathedral

> I love the church—its winged seraphim,
> its silver vessels and candlesticks,
> the lights, the icons and the pulpit.
> —C.P. Cavafy, 'In Church'

Bulky as our sin
the old Russian cathedral
floats like a treasure chest
above the regular sea
of liberated Tallinn.

No one's autonomous
among the shadow-spires
of candles, the broken bread
all in the one rhythm
affirming grief and solace.

Glimmer of vestments, staidness
of old clothes—this you'd find
in Caravaggio:
what of our hesitancy,
as of a mood unmade?

The candle-world rejoins
the city by descending
white steps—ad hoc tribunal
of the un-denizened
begging our euro coins.

Their pride an asset stripped,
their need a testimony
to the never-alien flesh,
their '*kiitos allelujah*'
a tampering with our script,

they summon us from beyond
time's rood into a new
picture. Can we pass by?
In smiles, all privilege
forgiven, we correspond.

Kiitos: Finnish for 'thank you'

The Kingfisher's Announcement

The hose is making true
circles on grass
among the bougainvillea,
amid announcements
by myna and pied kingfisher:
its wand augments the dew.
The cooking smells
will qualify cajew
and gardenia,
as the heavens turn blue.

If talent means, for things
that leave behind
the gravity of the familiar,
shall we, in travelling so far
for the kingfisher's announcement,
encounter a place jinxed,
questions tugging too hard
the roots of our own being?
Or in the vacancy,
acquire his wings?

We have the run of Goa;
yet seem to roll
between the promontories of home and here.
Among bath-towels and buggies
our children hardly know
how we've exposed
ourselves to the merely casual.
Sparrows meet kingfishers
on these warm strands
and half-prefer the cold.

Casement in Pentonville

Casement cribbed in Pentonville
in his narrow cell
prepares a last pilgrimage;
as if the iron bell

of an ancient monastery,
finding its way in
unbidden, sifts memories,
absolves all sin.

Something is made manifest,
bare to his bare soul.
There come crowds of dispossessed,
numbered in a roll

none had dared dream existed:
mutilated ones,
whom rubber bosses' twisted
discourse and clean guns

crushed, the cast-off instruments
of distant life-styles;
Amazonian Indians,
their barefooted files

no match for money-reckoning;
out of Ireland last,
those hidden, scattered remnants,
without king or caste.

These poor have no influence
and only stand by
to share the vigil, whom once
your cold chivalrous eye

acknowledged, hating misrule.
Comes there then One more:
Christ brooking no ridicule
batters at the door.

Disengagement

We thought that boundaries
to split the sun from shadow
would mollify,
neighbour turn neighbourly to neighbour,
our hectares of common ground subsume
the arid principalities;
until, one Monday morning in Salle B,
the Persian Gulf rolled in mind's eye:
a Rubicon, or else green fields,
a future to be attained
by laser-engaged ordinance
and pathways hateful to mothers.

Circumstances were beyond control,
the time for talk was over.
But someone asked
if the reported evidence
entitled one to make
a judgment wholly negative
on prospects for negotiation.
It seemed a self took shape,
and something composite
on which the hour depended
might almost rend.
And nothing was written down.

A man in his ebb-time—
for soon the message came
informing Chancelleries
that Foreign Minister Fernandez Ordoñez
was *very tired, very unwell*
and unlikely ever again to resume his functions.

For those with ears
for what is disconnected
from the giant mechanism
sprung, Leucippus said,
from atoms and the void,
the tolling bells of destiny
by an impromptu alteration
are strings and flutes—
a perfect psalmody,
yet carefree as goats' bells,
the medley of the many-footed flock
tripping pell-mell in shadow towards the fold.

The Great Maidan

My only sleepless night for Benazir
was not a claim on love, or not at least
under its major sub-heads; it came near
duty; yet somehow any duty ceased,
gone with her going, once the funeral
was over. So my anxious hesitancy
deriving from no rule was personal:
the matter grievous, the decision free.

And in the end I travelled. Plans abandoned,
I went on Internet and booked Finnair
and crossed a continent and seas to London.
Careful as other old friends gathering there,
I too had brought to that impromptu scene
late virtual roses for the laughing girl
of Lady Margaret Hall. The one you'd been,
the something in you that we all once were,

was then transparent in the character
and billboard face of representative.
Was there as well an anguish night would stir,
the day's work never settle? Ours to give
this journey for an elegy, to scan
in miniature your fateful exodus
and last appointment in the great *maidan*:
history that called on you was calling us.

A Judaean Diplomat Recalls
Year One

That he himself had played a useful part
was not, of course, the main point. Others too,
the lawyers, money-dealers, high officials,
knew what it took to end the humiliation
of the diaspora, of Pompey's conquest.
Their new Judaea had had her men at Rome,
was open to the world. The spectacles,
an enviable lack of pettiness
rewarding merit, their adroit life-styles—
all attributes of an effective state.

At Alexandria, the indolent
had wanted them to fail; for indolence
allows no greatness and desires no king.
Even at Rome (it never went as far
as Caesar or Agrippa) one picked up,
more delicately put, the same reserve:
cunning King Herod, Jewish roots forgotten,
was oscillating; round him, held by fear,
a changing clique; his co-existing gods
unable, somehow, to deliver the people.

And it was true, the formula they'd found—
it being no longer thinkable to live
by the old law—was never written in stone.
God was with Rome. Their options were surrender,
the dice-throw of defiance, or else this:

the hard path of engaging with the Romans.
Defining that most fortunate arrangement
was for a Ptolemy, a Nicolaus,
and those at court who knew Greek. Obscure claims,
legends of David's line, could play no part.

Until the census, this had all made sense.

Could there have been an option even then
for the well-informed to rise above the clamour
and stop the slide? For though Quirinius
measured in full the substance of the State
for tolls and taxes, Pilate's aqueduct,
just now complete, contended stone by stone,
one could survive the Romans. That unearned
bitterness of the young was mixed with lies.
He wished he could have bundled into phrases
his burning thoughts to pass them to the people!

He kept, of course, a city residence,
and places on the coast. But in all truth,
life was precarious. Where old state servants
revered her as a daughter, could protect
her somewhat, those who dreamt Jerusalem
naked, who shook off habits and dishevelled
fine schemes, were flashy and pointless: butterflies
oblivious of the times, their flimsy wings
beaming like oracles. Judaea was now
an unsteady platform, a disputed cause.

Varus, that force of nature, on the death
of Herod crucified two thousand of us;
in Galilee, slave-trader's bonds bit hard—
Varus, a boy beside the emperors!
Fortune has ridiculed our fathers' sons,
the knife-boys who conspire in silence—them,
and prophets in the sanctuary trailing
their hope, their cave-dust. Will fair words appease
touted insignia? Can we engulf
in silence the Antiochean cavalry?

The year Quirinius came, I call Year One.

In Ch'ang-an's Markets at the End of Spring

The hard-earned vantage of a patient mind
when it discloses beauty
deserves the name of poem.
Your poetry, Bai Juyi,
is a retreat and respite;
as when from spring to spring,
in fealty to Mount Lu's majesty,
you fitted your thatched hall
with wholesome things—
a bamboo trough, a corner for your books—
and under the great pines laid out white stones.

When Tara turns your page—
our little one so like your Golden Bells—
lost love, for whom you had endured
hard-won position,
its grit, gravamen—
you two shall walk, you in my place,
in Ch'ang-an's markets at the end of spring.

Tea-houses welcome you.
A music-maker with his lute
taps rhythm on the cassia-wood
and traces melody
on rose-red strings.
The whole room turns,
you join the singing:
songs worn like a garment,
songs to dispel
the micro-climates of dulled minds
by which the poor go hungry.

When Tara takes your book,
may she discover reasons of the heart
beyond locality
and jump the abyss of time!
May bales and spices,
the voices fresh from boats,
proclaim the import of this ornate world!

The Lute-Girl

after Bai Juyi

In dreams, he was a horseman through Ch'ang-an,
colleagues beside him, under falling snow.
In morning's heat, my friend was a sick man.
All day the waves would beat against the prow
of that hired skiff, and still he feared to start out—
to bite the bitter fruit of lifelong parting.

"A last red lotus flattened by the wind
won't share the bloom succeeding summers bring;
and on my journey south, I take no friend.
Returning to Mount Lu, I will climb, and sing,
and illustrate, as long as Time allows,
the streams that flee me and the evasive clouds."

The river eager, the moon at our disposal,
just as the last excuse for words was gone,
we heard lute-music. Quick, my old friend rose
in the unsteady skiff, and on my arm
clambered ashore; with no more words exchanged,
we sat within the sound's and the stars' range.

The lute-girl was veiled by reeds. Her tight-strung notes
were pearls or seed-pearls tumbling in a dish;
her after-silence, as the while she floated
nearer, was girded—steady as the wish
of spring as it unbuttons the ice's grip:
what new cascade of words might she let slip?

Her blossoming time in the imperial city—
through tears, her voice came darker than the river—
was filled with invitations: the bud so pretty,
no one took care of how the rose would live.
Rich men had followed her, and often turned her
with jewels, jests, and offers of rich journeys.

"On impulse then, a trade in the bazaar,
I took as husband a man I briefly knew.
Where tea-fields ripen, there his interests are:
the gold, the women of his retinue.
My life is lived: what is it then can move
such things my lute still whispers me of love?"

At this, my friend, embracing her with words,
cried out: "We vagrants without ceremony
live love as in a palace. We hedge-birds,
we weightless ones, take on our gravity
at such a time as this. Our pain recedes
when a pure lute is kindled in the reeds."

She raised her face, the very mask of beauty,
and sang once more, more softly now; he sat
as if to engrave the stories of that lute
on Time's own tablets. The stars' exeat
expired, the knowledgeable moon withdrew;
and his and my dark robes were laced with dew.

Ana Makes Ice-Cream

I FIND SOME notes I made, half-legible,
on Belgian delegation stationery—
from which I tell
it's nineteen ninety three,

Mandela has been released,
Major is British Prime Minister,
and Europe is astir
somewhere on the red piste

between Maastricht and Amsterdam.
And there at forty-one,
(according to my notes) I am,
learning how ice-cream's done.

THE AFTERNOON IS bright,
French windows open. Yolk and white
await a methodology
Ana's Aunt Naomi

has laid down: the Grand Marnier
to lower the freezing point; a counter strewn
with an array
of condiments; a wooden spoon;

the several bowls and whisks.
Before beginning,
Ana will pick out discs:
the Eurhythmics, Mozart, and Dame Vera Lynn.

SO WHAT BECAME of us? We could not know
the fate of Kosovo,
or that "securitised" would be the word
everywhere heard;

or picture how much worse
the universe,
viewed from our pied–a–terre,
would start to look—a minus here or there

dropped from equations, the globe's fall
would leave us all
nowhere. But from our nest,
we took both trouble and rest.

THE ONSET OF our love
all afternoon
was neither late nor soon.
No history written from above

or cold cosmology
will alter that day.
Ice-cream that melts too generously
will have its resumé;

as Naomi's
card-indexing of recipes
under an antebellum sun
is not undone.

Finlandia

Out of a landscape lean, near-binary,
whose lakes are panels brightening in the embrace
of moon or morning, where the pine-forests,
pillar and pediment above the silence,
are shadow-temples for a sword-less people,
is born the intimacy of our inflected
language, a song-source to which Goethe turns,
a *kantele* in midst of the assembly.

In these old songs, a military levy
is like forced marriage, a doing down of hope;
and when in time a modern Duchy is born
in swirls of war, our poet will prefer
the losers' camp. Not for a vagrant king,
absentee landlords, or the rent-seeking
nomenklatura, the ensign holds his ground:
under vain princes is achieved our good.

Engel's cathedral beckons to the harbour.
Helsingfors' libraries, academies,
so civil on the impertinent old rock,
chorus a coming change. What Edelfelt
and Halonen will paint, Sibelius
at Ainola discern, is inseparable
from Snellman in a stone chair overseeing
winter to snowy winter the main bank.

Then, in a totalising century,
what held together almost comes apart,
disproved in the great ordeal. To be sparing
of categories too clear for politics
is part of the new learning; how those means
more stern than Man—the barbed-wire camps, invasions,
hypotheses of necessary force,
of destiny—build nothing and lead nowhere.

The equation is not yet written to explain
our scapegoat, walled up, stiffening into age,
the Esplanade a tram-shuttle away,
who picks his *pitkospuut* across bog-days
for what he's a part of—Sundmalm's trees at autumn,
bow-windows by the brackish bay, the sea-ice
clenching its fist, the lilies of the valley
again in dialogue, time's un-graced womb.

At Hietaniemi, Marshall Mannerheim,
the dying Cú Chulainn of nineteen forty-four,
rests by the trusting and obedient ones; like kindling,
bunches of heather propped up at their graves;
candid, un-candid, a grey slate of sea,
a blade in the half-light; "Finlandia"
quicksilver in the rain. What flames will follow
in the old bonfire? And who desires the blaze?

Our comfort isn't stricken by an angelic
sorrow, by signs to be intuited
from the Great Bear, the surface of the lake
at Tuusula, the white walls of our churches.
Though ripening lore, a shaping intellect,
called us away, now ingenuity
connects us—our designs, our European
policy trellised on a constraining reason.

The planetary question will demand
more detailed argument in level-toned
assemblies. What if bells or a poet's harp
interpret for us a scrabbling far away
on empty plates? For if together, knees
on the hard floor, we stared out on the tundra—
were like the Russians as the wave of mad
Napoleon arched up—how should we pray?

kantele: in the Kalevala, a stringed instrument used by the bards
pitkospuut: duckboards laid on muddy ground to provide a path

Poetics II

As if a blushing girl, to steal
Catullus's comparison,
has hidden an apple in her gown
for someone, and it tumbles down,
and everyone is interested, is how,
in dreams, the publishing gets done.

Water is Best

Shining candles will be
Lit in each window
And a fire of turf
On each hearthstone kindled.

—Máirtín Ó Direáin
'Cuireadh do Mhuire' ('Invitation to the Virgin')

THIS LANDSCAPE JOGGED by the Atlantic,
her island-hood
nuanced by causeways,

wasp's bellies of stone, requires
no definition,
existed always.

That sudden flash on the Italian
website, the news
of some *ennesima*

strage, some umpteenth massacre,
a bomb has caused
in the Baghdad bazaar,

will not re-orient our day
persisting rainy
in Indreabhán. Our lens

to construe hope is un-performing
light on *carraig*
and *cloch* that no bomb rends.

SOME SAY THE PLENTEOUSNESS of time
in Connemara,
or when the hunger lays

tenuous fingers on bare slopes
around Darjeeling
or loiters in some haze

of Africa, is consequent
on a complete
conquest; as if the soul

fumbled both knives and reasoning.
But here, within
decorum, is the avowal

of what might be and of an old
story ignoring
noise and aggrandisement:

grey are the waters of the mind
when rulers read
reticence as assent.

THE CHEMICALS THAT FIX the colours
in blocks of cloth
produce a harsh excess

that in the aftermath requires
our counterpoise.
Nature is in distress,

we give support by engineering
Nature's own gifts
to make things right. We fix

a compost made of worms and ordure,
herbs and live plants,
above a filter, a mix

of stones, grit, sand. The noxious liquid,
faced by our feat
of reason, runs its course:

through the set strife of organisms
it flows purged,
cleansed by a natural force.

BUT WATER'S PUREST image must
rise up, a form
before the shaping eye,

if love with natural elements
is to combine
and dyes and dyes' dregs die.

The glittering mirror of salt sea
was dark, Odysseus
walked on with heavy oar:

others' indifference to that curve
and potency,
the sign he waited for.

*Beidh coinnle geala i ngach fuinneog
lasta*—Ó Direáin
has pictured for us how

candles could burn in every window
and wanderers
find welcome, even now.

Lightning Source UK Ltd.
Milton Keynes UK
19 October 2010

161573UK00001B/69/P